My Pet Sounds Off:
Translating the Beach Boys

poems by

Holly Painter

Finishing Line Press
Georgetown, Kentucky

My Pet Sounds Off:
Translating the Beach Boys

For Paul Legault, my best beach buddy

Copyright © 2020 by Holly Painter
ISBN 978-1-64662-205-4 First Edition
All rights reserved under International and Pan-American Copyright Conventions. No part of this book may be reproduced in any manner whatsoever without written permission from the publisher, except in the case of brief quotations embodied in critical articles and reviews.

ACKNOWLEDGMENTS

I gratefully acknowledge the editors of the journals in which these poems first appeared:

Barrelhouse: "I Get Around," "God Only Knows," "Wouldn't It Be Nice," & "Friends"
Collapsar: "Surfin' Safari," "409," & "Little Deuce Coupe"
Crack the Spine: "Good Vibrations"
The Museum of Americana: "Help Me Rhonda," "Barbara Ann," & "Caroline, No"
Specter: "Please Let Me Wonder," "When I Grow Up (To Be a Man)," & "California Girls"

Publisher: Leah Maines
Editor: Christen Kincaid
Cover Art: Emily Beam
Author Photo: Emily Beam
Cover Design: Elizabeth Maines McCleavy

Printed in the USA on acid-free paper.
Order online: www.finishinglinepress.com
also available on amazon.com

Author inquiries and mail orders:
Finishing Line Press
P. O. Box 1626
Georgetown, Kentucky 40324
U. S. A.

Table of Contents

1962
  Surfin' Safari
    Surfin' Safari 1
    409 2

1963
  Surfin' U.S.A.
    Surfin' U.S.A. 3
  Surfer Girl
    Surfer Girl 4
    Catch A Wave 5
  Little Deuce Coupe
    Little Deuce Coupe 6
    Be True To Your School 7

1964
  Shut Down, Vol. 2
    Fun, Fun, Fun 8
    Don't Worry Baby 9
  All Summer Long
    I Get Around 10
    Wendy 11

1965
  Today!
    Dance, Dance, Dance 12
    Help Me, Rhonda 13
    Please Let Me Wonder 14
    When I Grow Up (To Be a Man) 15
  Summer Days (and Summer Nights!!)
    California Girls 16
  Single
    The Little Girl I Once Knew 17
  Beach Boys' Party!
    Barbara Ann 18

1966
  Pet Sounds
    Wouldn't It Be Nice 19
    Sloop John B 20
    God Only Knows 21
    Caroline, No 22

1967
- *Smiley Smile*
  - Good Vibrations 23
- *Wild Honey*
  - Darlin' 24

1968
- *Friends*
  - Friends 25

1969
- *20/20*
  - Do It Again 26
  - Cotton Fields (The Cotton Song) 27
- *Single*
  - Break Away 28

1970
- *Sunflower*
  - This Whole World 29

1971
- *Surf's Up*
  - Surf's Up 30
  - Feel Flows 31

1972
- *Carl and the Passions—So Tough*
  - All This Is That 32

1979
- *L.A. (Light Album)*
  - Good Timin' 33

1985
- *The Beach Boys*
  - Getcha Back 34

1989
- *Still Cruisin'*
  - Kokomo 35

Surfin' Safari

C'mon, baby, it's time to surf.
Yes, right now! Get your stuff!
We're gonna be big game hunters of the sea.

We'll be there at dawn because we're that hardcore,
got our boards and some hotties in bikinis.
Now listen to this poppy tune:

Are you watching, girl?
We're surfing!

There're surfers at Huntington, Malibu, Rincon.
We'll be hunting for waves in the islands soon.
You'll come, too, woncha, baby?

Are you watching, girl?
We're surfing!

I know the names of some foreign places
if there's surfing there: Laguna, Cerro Azul, Peru.
Surfing's really taking off as a sport.

It feels good to be part of something bigger than myself.

Are you watching, girl?
We're surfing!

C'mon, baby, it's time to surf.
Yes, right now! Get your stuff!
We're big game hunters of the sea.

409

My car's like a woman
and she's unbelievably sexy.

I've been collecting coins
since the day I was born
saving up to buy my own 409.
And not a used one either.
This one's from the dealership.

Other cars are much slower.
They can't get near my car.
When I take her to the track, I'm especially proud.
When my 409 wins all the races,
I get to tell the other boys about her specs.

Go faster, you equine beauty!
Faster, faster, 409!
Faster, 409!
Faster, faster, 409!
Faster, 409!

Other cars are much slower.
They can't get near my car.

Surfin' USA

If the ocean was a thing
you could have on land
everyone would surf
like they do in California.
You'd be able to spot them
by their sun-bleached white-'fros,
Americans on surfboards.

You'd see them surfing in a number of places
including Del Mar, Ventura, Santa Cruz,
Trestles, Narrabeen over in Oz,
Manhattan Beach, and Doheny,
(although these are places
you can already surf).

We'll plan a road trip and wax our boards
and take off for the whole summer.
If our teacher should inquire
as to our whereabouts

tell her we're surfing.
We're Americans on surfboards.

Some other places you can already surf:
Haggerties, Swamies, Pacific Palisades
San Onofre, Sunset, Redondo Beach, L.A.
La Jolla and Wa'imea Bay

Everyone's surfing.
We're Americans on surfboards.

Surfer Girl

Little
        heart   undone

    love me,
        my little

                      shore
Standing by

    love me,
        my little

                surf
                    grow
my woody
Everywhere I go

              dreams come

Catch A Wave

Surfing makes you feel like a god.

Surfing's not that scary, I swear.
It's only the haters who won't even try it.
Just splash on out there, rotate 180 degrees,
and get ready for a wave to bring you back.
That's really it. It's not that complicated.

I'm telling you, surfing makes you feel like a god.

It's not like surfing's new.
The ancient Polynesians did it,
and now there's a growing population of surfers.
Even the critics will eventually be converted
and you'll see them all down at the beach.

And then surfing will make them feel like gods.

Get a talented surfer to give you weekly lessons.
A male surfer, obviously. A young man.
Maybe even me. I mean, if you want.
But promise me you'll take it seriously
and not just fool around on the beach.

Surfing makes you feel like a literal god.

Little Deuce Coupe

Hey babe, I'm being serious, so hear me out:
I drive the fastest car in the tri-county area.
When I'm stopped at a light, no one wants to race me
because this thing's like a rocket, but horizontal.

She's my old-timey Ford
and she's faster than you'd think.

She's just an old '32 with her original engine,
but she'll make your new Thunderbird appear stationary.
I've done a lot of work to her body, got her weight down,
so now she reaches a top speed of 140 mph.

She's my old-timey Ford
and she's faster than you'd think.

She has a ceramic clutch for increased friction
and an engine that's soft until I tell her to growl
and if you still don't believe me,
then let's race—winner take both cars.

She's my old-timey Ford
and she's faster than you'd think.

When the green lights up
she squeals and smokes off the line and
I'm nearly helpless to steer, what with the G force
blowing my cheeks all the way back to 1932.

She's my old-timey Ford
and she's faster than you'd think.

Be True To Your School

Whenever I hear some asshole
going on about how great his school is,
I jump in and tell him about my school,
which has both outstanding academics
and a competitive sports program.

I got my varsity jacket
for football and track
and I wear it everywhere
so other kids can see my school's name
and be jealous of me.

We really get pumped for football games
and contemplate doing lasting physical damage
to the opposing team's players.
My girlfriend's over there on the pep squad
cheering for me and the school.

You gotta to root for your school
just like she's your girlfriend.
You gotta to root for your school
and make sure everyone knows.

Fun, Fun, Fun

She asked to take the car
to the library, but instead
she turned up the radio, binged In-and-Out,
and drove considerably over the speed limit.

It'll be a pleasant afternoon
till Father repossesses the car.

The other girls are bitchy and jealous
because she's so stylish in that T-bird.
She drives so fast that, in comparison,
stockcars look like chariots.

It'll be a pleasant afternoon
till Father repossesses the car.

But it couldn't last forever.
Father saw you zipping around
followed by a pack of eager young men
and barred you from further use of the car.

But... I have a car?
And I'll drive you around
if you'll let me flirt with you.

And it'll be a pleasant afternoon
now that Father's repossessed your car.

Don't Worry Baby

I get these anxious thoughts all the time
like an echo chamber in my head.
I'm paranoid that something bad's going to happen.

But she holds my shoulders
and says, "Stop! You're being fatalistic."
and she says "Chill out, love."

Chill out, love.
Chill out, love.
There are no bears.

I probably shouldn't've been such a douche
telling everyone about my new car.
Now someone's challenged me to a race.
I don't want to, but there's quite a lot of peer pressure.

She gives me a pep talk
and when I start referencing crash statistics
she says, "Stop! You're being fatalistic."
And she says "Chill out, love."

Chill out, love.
Chill out, love.
There are no bears.

She tells me, "Look, when you're out there
racing around like an idiot, think of me.
I love you lots and you know
our love makes us immortal."

She's very persuasive
when she kisses me with enthusiasm
and she says, "Stop! You're being fatalistic."
And she says, "Chill out, love,"

Chill out, love.
Chill out, love.
There are no bears.

I Get Around

I drive in circles
I drive in circles
from girl to girl
and I have lots of sex.

I'm bored of my hometown
with its two stoplights and a post office.
I'm going someplace exotic and far-flung
but still accessible by land.

I belong to a clique that's been getting some press.
Now we don't have to deal with any menacing thugs.

I drive in circles
I drive in circles
from girl to girl
and I have lots of sex.

We ride in my car
because it gets the best mileage
and seems to attract women
for some reason.

None of us have girlfriends because they just get all pissy
when we ditch them on date night to drive in circles.

I drive in circles
I drive in circles
from girl to girl
and I have lots of sex.
Circles circles
Circles circles circles circles.

Wendy

Wendy, tell me what I did wrong.
You owe me that much
after all the time we had together.

I didn't know I could cry this much
until you cheated on me with that bastard.
Oh Wendy, you dumped me
and now I'm really sad.

Wendy, don't be stupid.
Forget this guy.
You don't know what you're doing.

I just don't see you two working out.
Don't you realize what a loser he is?
Oh Wendy, you dumped me
and now I'm really sad.

Come on Wendy, I wouldn't do this to you
'cause I'm a good person.
I used to think you were, too
but you probably never even loved me.

I was totally blindsided.
I thought we were happy.
Wendy dumped me.
Wendy, I'm really sad.

Wendy?

Dance, Dance, Dance

You know, my high school classes can be rather taxing
so I crank up the tunes for a bit of relaxing.

I need to dance, immediately, right where I am.
This song makes me hot.
So dance!

When people insult me I don't really mind.
My girl and my radio still treat me kind.

I need to dance, immediately, right where I am.
This song makes me hot.
So dance!

We never turn up at the start of a dance
but we'll really rock out when we get the chance.

I need to dance, immediately, right where I am.
This song makes me hot.
So dance!

Dance a lot, this song makes me hot.
Dance a lot, this song makes me hot.
Dance a lot, this song makes me hot.

Help Me, Rhonda

Since the break-up, I've been clinically depressed.
I stay out late drinking and spend all day in bed.
But Rhonda, you're a good-looking girl
and I feel like you could really expedite this process.

Rhonda, will you assist me
in getting over my ex?

We were engaged and everything.
I would've been a good husband
but then she ran off with the guy from HR
and now everything sucks forever.

But then, within a relatively short time span
I recovered enough to be horny again.
And that's when I noticed you, looking all cute,
and I can give you forty reasons why

Rhonda, you should assist me
in getting over my ex.

Please Let Me Wonder

I've been idolizing you and fantasizing
about the relationship we might have
for a long time now.

And that probably would've continued
but now we're actually talking
and I'm on the verge of hyperventilating.

But wait, don't tell me how you really feel.
Let me keep pretending you love me
as much as I love you.

I based my college decision, career, and hobbies on you
hoping we'd get closer if we had the same interests.
You can't imagine how much I hate artisan bread-making.

My idealized love and my idealized you
have become my life
and reality might kill me.

So don't tell me how you really feel.
Let me keep pretending you love me
as much as I love you.

When I Grow Up (To Be A Man)

My teen years won't last
Someday soon I'll be twenty
It's freaking me out

California Girls

Women from the East Coast dress well.
Southern women have charming accents.
Midwestern women are fully adequate.
Northern women give arousing kisses.

But I like Californian women best.
If it were possible
I'd like all women to be Californian.

West Coast sunlight results in marvelous tanning and
I'm into bikini-clad women on the beach under palm trees.
I've done a lot of travelling and met a lot of women
but I'm always eager to return home to my preferred sort of females.

I like Californian women best.
If it were possible
I'd like all women to be Californian.

The Little Girl I Once Knew

I didn't really fancy her until she hit puberty
but now she's positively smoking.
I want to get with her.

She is no longer a child
as she was when first we met.

Her preadolescent looks didn't predict her adult beauty.
I envy her boyfriend's proximity to her hot body.
I want to get with her.

She is no longer a child
as she was when first we met.

No, she's definitely not a child
as she was when first we met.

Barbara Ann

Barbara Ann, two things about you please me:

1. You arouse in me both lust and unsteadiness.
2. Your name is fantastically alliterative.

I met you at a school dance.
In my soul, there was a frenzy of attraction.

Again, I celebrate the wordplay your name inspires.

I did dance with some other girls that night,
namely Peggy Sue and Betty Lou

but I found that I couldn't scat sing their names
so I'll stick with you, Barbara Ann.

Wouldn't It Be Nice

I'm itching to graduate from high school
and shack up with you immediately.
Then everything will be perfect.

My grasp of what it means to be a grown-up
is tenuous and doesn't include
jobs, money, or responsibility.

I have this notion that adults
spend all day in bed having sex,
which is essentially my ideal.

What I'm picturing is sex before bedtime,
a good ten or eleven hours of sleep
during which we maintain close physical contact.

Then we wake up next to each other,
enjoy a quick chat about how beautiful the sky is
and follow that up with glorious morning sex.

I'm pretty happy with you now
but imagine if we could kiss continuously forever,
not even stopping for bathroom breaks or rehydration.

This is something I fantasize about constantly.
I even try to enlist God's help occasionally
by throwing in some mumbo-jumbo about marriage.

I know that obsessing about our imaginary future
and discussing it ad nauseum in the school cafeteria
is just a way of torturing ourselves in the present

but that's probably not going to stop me
from developing unrealistic expectations
and sharing them with you at every opportunity.

Sloop John B

      grandfather and me

           fight

So

                  sail
          Captain

I want to go home

                  drunk
And broke

                    and

                  alone

So

                  sail
          Captain

              let me go home

              I want to go home

    poor
And

                    ate up

              let me go home

So

                  sail
          Captain

              let me go home

God Only Knows

As long as some critical number of
celestial bodies remain visible in the sky
I'll be in love with you.
And I'll remind you often
usually in the form of a Top 40 song.

Only our Creator can say for certain
what would become of me if I didn't have you.

If you were to become disenchanted
with our relationship and end it
I would not commit suicide
but I would be very tempted
because you are all that gives my life purpose.

Only our Creator can say for certain
what would become of me if I didn't have you

but I can speculate, if you like:

I might be shooting up in the bathroom of a casino.
I might be carving driftwood into tears at the beach.
I might be attending a basketball game wearing glitter bodypaint.
I might be searching Grindr for baby bears.
I might be reading my poetry to the birds in the park.
I might be watching food-themed Japanese pornos.
I might be driving 150mph along the Nebraskan highway.
I might be tattooing your face on my stomach myself.
I might be running for office on an anti-panda platform.
I might be contemplating the existence of parallel worlds.

But really, only our Creator can say for certain
what would become of me if I didn't have you.

Caroline, No

Caroline, you seem to have made
some rather major life changes
possibly for your own betterment
but I don't like your new haircut.

You can't be operating autonomously.
Someone must have forced this on you
because you always used to tell me
that you would never, ever change.

This situation is highly distressing to me
and I find myself on the verge of tears.
Your inevitable maturation is an affront
to all of us who liked you better as a girl.

Will you ever again be the person I once knew?
Is there anything left to love about you?
Can I infantilize you back into adolescence?
I suppose not, not when you're this far gone.

Good Vibrations

I'm impressed by her vibrant dress sense
and the golden hue of her hair in the summer.
Her voice is soft and lovely when she utters niceties.
Her fresh, intimate scent wafts in my direction.

It turns me on like a seismograph.
She resonates so pleasantly
in my heart, mind, and groin.

With eyes closed, I feel connected to her.
Her mouth moves in the gentlest way
and when we make eye contact again
she joins my flowering fantasies.

It turns me on like a seismograph.
She resonates so pleasantly
in my heart, mind, and groin.

I am overcome by happiness,
astral projected somewhere incredible.
The sensation cannot be described.

I don't want this to end.
Let's echo forever
in this synesthetic dream.

Darlin'

My love,
guess what I did last night?

I learned how to write rhyming couplets
and then, I went on Wikipedia
and found a list of clichés
followed by a list of expressions
not used since 1950.

Guess who's working on a new poem...

Friends

We perform the functions of friendship well

both generally: having fun together, being supportive, introducing each other to new interests, maintaining the friendship over time, cheering each other up when life's hard,

and specifically: advising the other when a partner is cheating, lending each other money so everybody's solvent, mediating intense family disputes regarding personal grooming.

Long live our friendship.

Do It Again

I'm feeling nostalgic for my teenage years.
The past is sun-drenched, fleshy, wet,
full of beautiful California girls whose
hair alone made me feel content.
I remember all the surfing and dancing we did.

I miss you guys.

We should really get together sometime.
Somebody start a group text.

Cotton Fields (The Cotton Song)

I recently decided I'm a Southerner
and picked up this speech affectation
that suggests the people of Louisiana
speak English poorly.

All I'm really trying to do is tell you a story
about how I'm from a cotton plantation
in Louisiana, and one day, I got a flat tire and
had to get directions from a stranger.

I also want you to know I value you
above cotton, in case you were wondering,
and also, it's very hot in Louisiana,
hotter even than California at times.

I miss the cotton fields sometimes, so I go home
and it's great being back in Louisiana
especially seeing all the people I used to know
who are always surprised how much I've grown.

Break Away

Goodbye Capitol Records.
We've had enough of you.
We're going to do our own thing.

We can't keep waiting
for you to get your act together
and promote us properly.

Everyone who passed us by before
while you were dicking around
is listening to our music now.

That's why we're not worried.
We can break away from you
and have a better life.

At first, we thought
we were just being paranoid
but, no, you really are a bad label.

So we're leaving you
and we're suing you
and it feels really good.

This Whole World

The world is full of love
and people in love.

People split up sometimes
but often, they sort it out.

You are alive and free
and every day, you love me.

I am overcome by love
and must make telegram sounds.

Surf's Up

I'll bet you thought this would be
another happy-go-lucky surf melody.

Wrong.

Welcome to my dream
of diamonds and aristocracy,
batons and pendulums,
dominoes and columns.

What say you, Dr. Freud?
Am I really sleeping?

I see velvet curtains and chandeliers
in a music hall of
trumpets and swans.
The music dissipates at dawn.

What say you, Dr. Freud?
Am I really sleeping?

Among silver moons and doves,
Victorian gas-lamps and fog,
carriages and lofty spires,
a New Year's song in the cellar,

gulp of wine, and blazing fire,
the docks of many a drink,
grief that swells and chokes,
a tearless man already broken.

Crest the tidal wave,
ride with the young,
the naïve, the syrupy fools.
They sing a child's tune.

Children father men,
play harmonics of love,
and are never lost.
That's why children father men.

Feel Flows

Here, we show off our facility
with assonance, alliteration, and internal rhyme.

This song is brought to you by the letter W.
I summarize briefly:

Memories are hazy.
Sometimes we can access them.
Sometimes we can't.

We remember emotional times.
Hope and faith may soften this
or we can forget by sheer will.

Sleep shuts down our senses.
We may forget, we may remember.
We may be healed.

All This Is That

Well this is awkward.
We were supposed to be
the most popular band in America

until those British boys turned up.
A decade on, we've picked up their themes
and we're selling ourselves as knockoffs.

But it's okay because we are all one.

In the morning
I meditate on Robert Frost.

The goddess grants me happiness,
love, wisdom, and eternity.

What would Robert Frost
have thought about Buddhism?

Everything is one.

Auras replace shadows.
We are full of love.

Why didn't Robert Frost use surfing metaphors?
They can be very spiritual.

We are one.

Hail the divine guru
and the Beatles too.

Good Timin'

If there were a product called Good Timin'
this would be its jingle.

First, introduce the product name:
Good Timin'

Next, advertise its quality:
Good Good Timin'

And now, emphasize its necessity:
You need Good Timin'

Add a brief meditation on life in general:
Everyone's alive and getting educated...

and bring us back to the product:
...about Good Timin'

Reiterate necessity:
You need Good Timin'

And more musings on the state of humanity:
Everyone's alive together

Personal endorsement:
I love Good Timin'

Affirmation:
Yeah good Good Timin'

Final nonsense syllables:
Dow dow
Dow dow dow
Dow dow
Dow dow dow dow

Getcha Back

I heard our song on the radio
for the first time in a long time
and thought about how we broke up
because I kept pressuring you to have sex with me.

Do you think we could ever be together again?

I keep thinking about your new boyfriend
He's probably rich, handsome, and maybe even
nice to you, but he'll never love you as much as I do.
If I leave my girlfriend and you leave your boyfriend

do you think we could ever be together again?

Kokomo

The Caribbean appeals to me as a place
where we can get wasted on the beach
and have a lot of sex.

We can fly down there and relax
while drinking girly drinks, island-hopping,
and listening to the locals play their music.

I propose the following itinerary:

Aruba, Jamaica, Bermuda, Bahama
Key Largo, Montego, Martinique, Montserrat
Port au Prince, and of course, Kokomo.

Holly Painter's first full-length book of poetry, *Excerpts from a Natural History*, was published by Titus Books in Auckland, New Zealand (2015). An MFA graduate of the University of Canterbury in Christchurch, she teaches writing and literature at the University of Vermont.

Holly's poetry has been published in literary journals around the world, including *Barrelhouse*, *The Cream City Review*, *Bombay Gin*, and *Spork*. She is currently working on a book of poetry based on cryptic crosswords and a non-fiction interview project about obsolete jobs. Find out more at *hollypainter.com*.

www.ingramcontent.com/pod-product-compliance
Lightning Source LLC
LaVergne TN
LVHW041556070426
835507LV00011B/1114